Shy

poems by

Theresa Hickey

Finishing Line Press
Georgetown, Kentucky

Shy

ACKNOWLEDGMENTS

The following poems have appeared in these publications:

Apples from the Garden; Old Country~~*Still Point Quarterly, Shanti Arts*
Empty Nest~~*Halcyon Days*
Words~~*FaithND*—Notre Dame University
Gray Day~~*New England Memories*
Something about Trees; Of Water and Sea~~*Nature Writing*

Other poems by Theresa Hickey have appeared in *Raising the Child, Sighs of
a Gracious Nature. Sextant, N Magazine* and *The Naples Sun Times*.

Publisher: Leah Maines
Editor: Christen Kincaid
Cover Art: Photo by Alexandru Zdrobău on Unsplash
Cover Design: Elizabeth Maines McCleavy

Printed in the USA on acid-free paper.
Order online: www.finishinglinepress.com
also available on amazon.com

Author inquiries and mail orders:
Finishing Line Press
P. O. Box 1626
Georgetown, Kentucky 40324
U. S. A.

Table of Contents

Synopsis

Shy

*All I have seen teaches me to trust the Creator for
all I have not seen. Ralph Waldo Emerson*

*All I am becoming teaches me to trust the Creator for
all I am to be. Theresa Hickey*

Whether we are parenting, in the workplace, or discerning choices to be made, we may second-guess ourselves; we are not always sure-footed. I believe defining glimpses nudge us toward a more steady landscape. A centered home can become our reality as we realize that we have no desire for a life that is frenzied and unsatisfying. As we trust the spirit within, we are rejuvenated—able to persevere in attaining meaningful goals. With a little effort, we can learn how to pause—be silent—notice the extraordinary amid the commonplace, become better listeners and avid participants in life.

Every day there are grace-filled experiences in our lives that compensate for our deficiencies—ways to fill every void that seems to surface as we attempt to engage in the ebbs and flows of living. All we need do is open our eyes to them and trust in their benevolence. Sometimes that's easier said than done, but the greater power within us—whatever we believe that to be—knows what we need when we need it.

Featured in *Shy* are short poems about various and compelling forces—guideposts designed to shun fear and choose life in the decisions we face. I believe that this is, in part, Nature's plan—to be a steady source of resourcefulness. People, too, often come to our rescue with an encouraging word, something new to be learned or a welcoming remark. When we are open to these brief encounters, they enable us to move forward with greater confidence. We see more clearly how to walk in the world as the unique emissaries we are meant to be. We often think we are "shy"—that we fall short of all that we need to chart a purposeful and promising course for ourselves, but we deceive ourselves if we believe this.

Often, the poems of my *Shy* collection remind me that when I breathe more confidently from creative energy, I am in touch with a source meant to uplift. It takes a lifetime to familiarize ourselves with life lived in union with spirit. Yet, grace and confidence *are there*—lying in wait within—ready to rise from dormancy to fill the shy and empty spaces we need to enrich our own lives and to serve one another.

~ Theresa Hickey ~

Apples from the Garden

What does it mean to have a crazy old heart
thumping inside and a mind that's a bit singed
around its edges or what some say is a daft sense of
what is real? It comes about
when one loves and loses
or loves and prays for change
but change does not come . . . It comes about
as one loves and learns a few things but only
a few so that the soul continues its search
for light and truth, come what may.

When we are young,
everyone tells us to take a bite out of life . . .
we need to know . . . . *we really need to know,*
so we struggle and risk, adopting all
the ideas that we think help us grow
but instead, we become like Eve,
in her little garden.

When no longer children, is it then
okay to not know? When life changes
course, can we be content
to become lost along the way?
learn to till our own special soil?
turn our backs on all the things we
thought were "green" or "golden"
. . . learn to till our own special gardens?

Maybe this time we adapt
to a crazy old heart
thumping inside and a mind that's a bit singed
around its edges, with what, some say,
is a daft sense of what is real
because . . .
now we can strip down
lay bare the worms
taste the delicious fruit
every apple holds within its flesh.

A Small Exchange of Peace

Outside the nursery
a street lamp
illuminates this corner of the room
where you drift off in slumber;
your face, a moonbeam
bathed in wonder
on this starry night

One day your gaze
will scan the heavens
in search of something more;
you will want to grasp all
that twinkles in the sky;
I may want to place them
at your feet. Much
that shines in the universe
is not worth keeping; few things
hold promise beyond dreams

Tonight God binds the two of us
together to form a quilt of
life and love—threads
of giving, receiving. Knit
as one at birth and
in this moment's silence,
it is as if a weary world
depends upon
our small exchange of peace

Believers . . .

see countless things we miss
that shape the world of poets
who see life as a kiss
from the Creator

Something of His passion
shows up in ways that strive
to make them turn the other cheek
when hurt collides with hope

It is the tiny seed that flourishes
beyond the worldly pale—the child's hand
that lends assurances, as does
nature's tiny details

When death is near,
and grief abides, they give us
pause to understand
that God is only goodness

and by his love makes sweet
our time of leaving.
Though some of life is over
new life arrives to knock

upon the doors of every
open heart who is
willing to go forth to
praise his God

Take courage and do not buckle
in this season of our lives
for God holds us in his palm,
guides us to realize that death

Is kind and freeing when we have
lived and tried, and even if we disbelieve,
His death has made it right, so
all may cross from mystery to enter Paradise

Condolences

There is something about a loved one's dying
that causes us to tremble
when their heartbeat drums inside our chests—
when the tremor in our throats
gives rise to words
once spoken between us like prayers,
when sunsets melt each memory into night.

Until we meet again,
days of grain and harvest
accompany grief as it spreads
its wings toward the moon
or some other sanctuary
where unanswerable questions fly
seeking to be understood
and every poem of devotion
remains short of breath. When will tears
shed for the beloved
fill the parched desert with
an oasis that quells the thirst?

Something about death
makes me want
to capture sun's rays
in a velveteen purse. . . to plant a sapling. . .
to coax the infant
from its cradle. . . to live . . . to
live each day and not be afraid
to die a little bit
each morning—each evening
because in the end—
a promise has been pledged to us—

We will see each other again

Cradle Song

When no one's there to listen,
with little hesitation,
the buoyant sea embraces
like a mother. Fiercely wild
quietly calm
her empathy swells to heights
we soar, depths we plunge;
she rocks us

Her face beams
sunlight of a breaking morn
moonlight of a starry night—
rays of countless dawns and dusks
borne high upon her brow.
We wade releasing worries
to her winds; sanguine babes
in her arms; we rock

"Do not give up; do not give in."
Maternal lyrics speak
courage in her throes,
while waves of
Spirit graces fill the currents
of our days with hopes
that crest and flow;
she rocks us

One day when we are gone
and sadness bends itself to mourn,
the sea's same whispers fly
to loved ones as they weep. If
they listen closely,
a mother's peace will rise
as they seek comfort
in her prayer-lullabies;
"Rock on,
Rock on"

Dappled Days

The grandeur of sky and sea is awesome, but
in an orchard, one notices
small wonders

Each turn of weather
bears fruit, cleaving to the vines
clinging for clemency from storms

Dimpled valentines of berries,
tiny jewels—red and radiant
black and blue—fill baskets

Pierced in their prime, flushed
pinks and reds, noble nectars flow
from peaches, plucked from branches

In autumn, apples line rows of meadows;
succulent still, as once to Eve, the apple's
robust beauty tempts each hidden desire

Hardy seeds become the fruit of life
and we, our sight and taste reborn
from fertile soil the farmer tills,
are awed in silent ways
as we eat our fill
as we offer thanks and praise
for dappled days

December's Children

Dedicated to the families of the Sandy Hook Elementary School children who died on 12/14/12

It is
December, after all, but instead of singing strains of
"peace on earth, good will to men,"
there is only silence and a hush that lingers in the air.

The silence speaks of
Charlotte
Daniel
Olivia
Josephine
James
Ana
Dyland
Madeleine
Catherine
Chase
Jesse
Grace
Emilie
Jack
Noah
Caroline
Jessica
Avielle
Benjamin
Allison

It is
December, a time of miracles,
but for those who miss these little ones, there is no end
to questioning: *Where is the beauty,*
of the season when seemingly there is no light?—
yet somehow in the aftermath, The Spirit praises
their childlike joy and innocence.

It is
December, after all, and much has changed
for those remaining, and we,

the living, every one,
now pause upon the edge of time
to become a little more like these
born of purity and peace
until our journey brings us
to the home we all will share.

Absent for now
ever-present are their faces
in every other winter's presence
for after all,

It is
December . . . a time we herald love
that must never be postponed
or stored away, as there may never be
another hour, another day.

Doubt

I want to see the world with a piercing eye,
hold it in my palm, envision it in ways
that bring me to my knees.

Yet, if harsh words fly
like gulls, passing from my soul
to another without remorse, how
will I find peace?

What if I neglect to
express regret for an opportunity
missed, become indifferent
or indignant
instead of offering praise?

How can I notice the hidden,
embody the benign and beautiful,
sear the memory
with words, if
mindfulness falls dormant
over time?

It is in the twilight's stillness,
the Spirit sings in harmony and sends
with it the morning light
to flush my cheeks
soften my fickle heart—lends
courage to begin anew,
as if among the earth's newborn,
sent to hover . . .
to discover—
no matter how often
I may tell myself
there is nothing new to write, there is
nothing more to say . . . I may never
become like the poets I hold dear . . .

Empty Nest

Across rooftops, chimneys
of brick and copper cupolas
amid spindley branches
is a thickness in the trees—
a perfect nest . . .
I see it now, intertwined
with branches that must have
always been a safe haven
for birds, but I
had never noticed it
until you went away.

Now with summer's greenery fading—
the howl of autumn winds
shake down the leaves
from every tree limb;
the nest is easier to spot
above the bleak landscape.

The nest withstood
strong northeast gales
that chilled the woods 'til April
but for those who raise a child
months come and go
without much notice
of the seasons' cues and rhythms.

It's only on a day like this
when suddenly
realization dawns
that things must change—
that those at home accept
the old familiar place
without the one familiar face
that's always been there
and begin looking
to the birds
for consolation.

Eulogy

Today,
I hear a much-loved artist
talk about the passing of someone
with whom he'd created
memorable music. Remembering, he said:
"I miss him as one might miss the rain."

Great Fish

Hail to you high flying, spirited
fish—your silvery torso leaps
as if to catch a morsel in mid-air
instead of becoming the morsel
to be hooked
to be snared
caught on the line
of the bony-kneed boy
whose fingers snag bait
whose reel flails
with the utmost confidence
like the whip of a lion tamer

Before your quick reentry to the sea
your scales shimmer in the sun;
a glint, a flash,
a momentary badge of courage
defines your display of rebellion.
Only for an instant
do I catch that arc
that refined thrust
that fierce curve of your spine
but I know
your determination
your daring to be free

Gray Day

Raindrops chime against
a metal watering can left outdoors
among seedlings, yet to be planted;
unopened bags of loam
lie neglected,
stacked obelisks awaiting sun.

As rain ripples, begins to pool,
it gathers in gutters
along the potting shed
before cascading
in sheets along matted ground.

I sip morning coffee, lukewarm,
cool feet against smooth surfaces of tile,
eyes, not quite alert from rivers of sleep,
ideas, slow-rising from dormancy.
What lies ahead from this infant-of-a-day?

A clocks ticking insists on flicking
immediacy upon the present.
Should I go off to perform rituals,
begin gardening when the sky
clears, check items from a list?

I want only to remain here,
to look out my window—
embrace this small contentment
dwelling in the quiet
before contending
with a less-than-perfect world.

Dance of the Butterfly

Nature releases butterflies
    to wake us from our sleep
        so that dreams may be born

Tiny emissaries,
    seemingly of little consequence,
        invite us to envision peaceful possibilities

With delicate thrusts, they
    propel motion—buoyantly,
        as though possessing heavenly spirits

They float and career over rocks
    and ridges, grasses and flora, darting just as sprightly
        long dusty roads as green meadows

Soaring ever so lightly from the ordinary
    into the realm of the magical, their ethereal presence
        reveals the grace of a grander scheme

As I child,
    I tried to capture butterflies in a net, contain them
        in a jar; their frail wings did not give me pause

to imagine how fragile their flight—
    how wrong my attempts
        to snatch them from the landscape

Rising skyward above green trees
    or alighting on the dew-grass of summer
        the message of the butterfly is carried to the earthbound:

~ Living is a delicate freedom ~

Love Letter from Paul

Love is patient, love is kind" *
        and ... Love should always
        speak when it is sorry ...

Silence can be a warm embrace
        where nothing necessary
        need be said or written,
        nothing need be shared,
        not a word
        or an utterance of a thought

but there is also a silence that cripples
        constricts our cores
        like stings of swarming bees, a sign
        to make amends before separation
        isolates. It can paralyze,
        as trapped we become
        like mummies in a tomb;
        ultimately its weight shatters
        like fragile glass

A good friend,
        silence reveals our sorrows
        when time is right
        if we examine as physicians do
        the reasons why we hurt ...

Whenever the heart is heavy
        it may be we've harmed another
        and surely it is time to say,
        "I'm sorry." Indisputably
        as this happens, peace will
        overtake us, and the love
        that we are slow to give
        pours down again like rain

*1st Corinthians, 13:4

Love: Where Do You Go?

The inscription on his stone read,
"In the end, it is love that lasts"

But on the ordinary days
when nobody paid attention,
was it on his lips, in his mind,
on his heart, in his steps?

If so, perhaps this wife, these children,
all gathered around to say goodbyes,
may have had a glimpse
of it, known it to be true,
claimed it as their own:

In the end, love *will not* die

In the end, it weaves its way
like a river, past the eulogies
in the oratory, past the days of loss
and grief, resilient in hearts
where it's been planted

Heat lightening in the wake
of a storm, love illuminates
the night, purifying
visions, purging sorrows
with a fire that brands the flesh

No . . . love does not die
but chisels us towards a new beginning,
breakthroughs of the mind and heart.
Like a young bride and her husband
on the threshold of new life;
like an infant at the breast,
a passion fills our veins again
because love heals,
raises the dead
endures

Nativity

Born within my center is
an inn i call my home, where
all is quiet without grief
where realities of death and war
elude me, where i search
once for all, for peace.
When tragedies ensue,
exhaust and fill me,
when broken dreams
are daunting in the night,
when people disappoint
and eyes betray me, i
rest within
the cradle of my birth

Sadness and remorse
may break my spirit,
hurled arrows through the air
aim at my mind
but from the potter's wheel i'm
bent and shapen, reborn to
lend compassion toward mankind.
Each disappointment is
as from a razor; i am slow
to embrace the bitter with the sweet, but
poured freely from life's pitchers
are fresh waters
to bathe me in the temple
of my own nativity

Needy

A misguided world thinks that
poets are sages—that they know some things
the rest of us don't;
but poets—are misfits—
who know they know
nothing, so they sift
for gold nuggets
from a panhandler's cup.
Unlike earth's
gem stones—emeralds
or sapphires—only in deeds
do one's words catch the light.

Locked in the silence
as they skim the lake's surface
with tiny, flat pebbles that ripple
the pale, they step upon cracks
the world tries to jump over
doling out tears
as "the first stone" is hurled. Like
hot coals—there's a spark—
there's a glimmer—
a prayer in the darkness
to dispel one's fears.

They lend us a child's mind
to lead us, to wean us, to float
us to islands or places of rest
but they—the world's beggars—still restless,
still searching— bleed along with us,
barefooted and frail. When they
stumble on secrets, hard hearts
are then broken, it is then that
words become manna—like
bread at a meal.

Beautiful dreamers, they seek
earthly treasures in canyons,
in crators, in caverns of clay. When
a prophet says, we are blind
we are lame—"we are rocks"
says the poet who owns the thick boulder
that blackens his eye.

Of Water and Sea

We, who dot
            the parched land, need oceans
                        of resiliency to sustain prevailing winds
                                    that we might grow in courage
                                                that we might not grow old
                                                            before our time

We watch as tides
            come in-go out, but rarely do we
                        seek the comfort of the sea
                                    to show us mercy, refresh us
                                                so that dreams do
                                                            not run dry

Breathe in—absorb her wisdom,
            each ebb and flow spills out a melodic mantra—
                        a universal mother,
                                    she carries off upon her crests
                                                the fears a cynical world provokes—
                                                            as we breathe out

With every breaking wave,
            each shift of current washes us
                        as we become reborn
                                    destined to become her children—
                                                powerful
                                                            free

Old Country

Mixing water and mortar
my father poured concrete
for a pathway to his garden—
skills he learned
from my grandfather
in his native Italy.

An early childhood memory
was watching as he planted,
beads of sweat seeping
from the furrows
of his temples,
shoulders, neck—
his suntanned face,
russet as the pears
of his beloved fruit trees.

Outstretching a sturdy arm
across the picket fence
he'd stop to rest a while,
surveying his abundance—
peppers, squash, tomatoes—
some yet to ripen,
not quite ready
to be plucked.

Tweaking the center
of his mouth, he honored
their perfection—
"Delizioso!" was his
daily compliment
as he blew to them
his kisses—his passion
always present;
his animation—
a source of joy.

After a repose,
he'd gather up
ripened vegetables for soups—
packing some in
small, brown bags

for delivery to neighbors.
This was his summer ritual
from which I learned
to share.

In the fall—so rare figs
might fully sweeten,
he pruned back tough
tree branches, wrapping ends
and roots in burlap
before cool nights set in.

Then he built
a sturdy woodshed
for the tree's protection,
completely encircling it
to survive harsh winter
snowfalls that would kill it
if it were to be exposed.

Such an oddity was this
wooden box—
a source of much
embarrassment when questioning
neighbors wondered
who or what
was buried there.

It wasn't until he died
that images of his fig tree
wound 'round inside my head,
often leading me to his garden
to offer silent prayers.

It is there
that I still find him
as I pause
before his blue madonna
in the thick green grasses
he had always mown
with the most,
meticulous of care.

On Creativity

It's an uneasy place in the middle,
when two dispositions arise
a conundrum of gargantuan proportions
makes us anxious— with no place to hide

No rest for the weary, it has often been said
of the one who is riddled with doubt;
part of the dilemma as humans—
discerning what angst is about

No place to run to; no time to tarry;
until *it is* done,
until *it is* done

It is time for a change when we're restless
Is there something we're having to do?
wet paint on the brush of an artist—
the creation of something brand new

It can be idea or action
encircling our minds like a storm
only when we step into its torrents
can the infant inside us be born

Rice and Beans

Long ago on desert plains
the One who walked on water
served a meal of bread and fish
to travelers who, once they ate it,
fed the rest—but I . . .
I stop long enough to visit
on this first trip to Haiti—
shake hands with those
who run an orphanage
pat the shoulder
of a little one who devours rice and beans
I serve; I do not know his name.

In City Soleil
at day's end, I find rest, but children
squatting in the square
do not; they have no shoes—
they have no toys—
their bellies of rounded emptiness
reflect in contaminated
pools of water where they play—
hunger is their mantra;
they need so much more than
rice and beans I serve;
I do not know their names.

I move about freely
where I come from—
green everywhere—grasses, trees.
I come from hope—from optimism—
from excess, but here in Haiti
there is little embracing of big dreams
only a daily ration of rice and beans.

I look
into muddy cesspools—
the pig styes
where the people live—
and wonder. . . . . Do they live
as they do because an indifferent world
does not care to know their names?

Small Wonders

May the wind-force surround you,
penetrate with a dynamic mind
protect you and the couple that conceived you
that none may fear the future,
you will grow as goodwill flows—
around, within you—
nursing with comfort
like a lullabye:
May no bad dreams, no bad thoughts pervade you;
only good dreams—good thoughts all your days

As the wind defends you, swiftly may
encouragement alight
upon your shoulders;
whisper its prayerful hymns; root you
in goodness, laughter and strength;
draw simple pleasures, good friends

A fortuitous force—may the wind
whisk away
each callous comment
each slanderous word spoken by assailants,
assist you to resist
each misguided whim —
for you, little one—
were seduced by love,
to embody and dispense it
born of stars and seas and skies
to see the universe
through God's eyes

Something about Trees . . .

brings me to my knees.
When they are greenest
joy buds with their foliage;
deepest hues set summer tables
rich with fruit, so sweet—
so ripe with possibilities

For a time,
autumn seeks attention in all
her flamboyancy. But when leaves fall,
last rights are dispensed so
not one bit of hubris remains

Though memory retains each bough
and image of a summer's day,
embryonic grays cannot be denied
when winter hovers

In winter's isolation, trees lie
in empathy of the earth-bound
silently awaiting rays of sun
silently awaiting change

One day when we draw closer
 to the roots of trees
in readiness
to depart the familiar

they will be
our confidantes as we
hide amid ethereal branches
to catch the coolness of their shade

As loved ones pass by
unaware, trees will murmur to them
so they may lose themselves
amid their outstretched arms,
believe in our rebirth

The Fisherman's Poem

Along the pier's weathered planks they cast hopeful glances—
their eyes, their lines fixed on the sea

Their tackle boxes boast feathery lures;
hooks, cutting tools to fillet the day's catches

Crusted along thick pilings are scraps of clinging mollusks,
vestiges of sordid sealife

Schools of fish play in these waters, silhouettes
against diminishing sun

For some, many fish are caught this day; for others
few, but for those who search the sea and sky

Gulls overhead form
a victory sign at the end of day—

A reward for the steadfast who trust the Lord,
says Mathew—
"Come after me, and I will make you fishers of men."*

These words are poem, prayer, philosophy

"Be patient and wait upon the Lord."

*Mathew 4:19

Tea and Eucharist

These were her favorite tea cups—
displayed throughout her china closet;
dainty floral cups of various shapes and colors
some with fluted edges—frail, with tiny petals

forming delicate patterns around the rims
they scarcely held a sip;
others featured sheaths of wheat
or sprays of lavender bouquets
forget-me-nots of blue.

On the nights she was ill
my mother needed to know
i loved her, but words never came
easily, so always—i brewed tea.

Sometimes she'd prefer
earl gray, sometimes camomile
steeped long inside the pot
poured out when piping.

Glancing at her grand collection—
a fine array of china from places
to which she never traveled
but purchased at St. Joseph's church bazaars—
tonight there would be musings to be shared—

Tonight before i stop
to count the pills, pay bills
and bring in groceries,
i envision what life might have been
without her and tell her of my thoughts.

I talk about the family
how she had enriched our lives
by interacting as she did
with each and every one—
how some of us are bold and bright
like the cups
displaying fuschia peonies
others light and mild

as buttercups, daffodils—

Still other family members
much more centered, they
are like the sturdy greens
of leaves and stems,
less like the garish blossoms
strewn across the matching plates.

Other nights, we affirmed
the other's presence
ushering in a more tranquil spirit—
with quiet rising holier than our voices
connecting us profoundly
in ways we dared not speak.

In the end, i revered these times
of ritual, though rarely
had i welcomed them
often merely passing through them
out of duty and respect.

Looking back, i am now comforted
by the calming kitchen vigils
by the ways we'd raise our cups
with regal poise.

I did not know then as we
chatted in her dimly-lit kitchen
that all-too-soon those same
small cups would become
my very own; i could not know

I would come to cherish
all the stories of her past
the ones she used to talk about
on those nights as we sipped tea.

The Actor

Never having acted before
in a professional capacity
I thought it ironic
when the director chose me

Once the run of the play was over—
the anticipation, the intensity, the lure
of the unexpected fulfilled—only one
lingering impression remained:

I was ecstatic
when people remembered
the character I portrayed and
nobody remembered my name

The Promise

Everyone mingles beneath a canopy
flashing broad smiles—

a lush landscape boasts pastel hollyhocks;
upon each linen-lined table, bud vases

filled with daisies, baby's breath; rows of
delicate pastries, fluted cups

of fruit, like tiny trumpets.
Steaks sear, spatter onto

red-hot coals. Wine flows—bubbles
sparkle in each glass, like gold;

white candles glow, dispensing
peace into a perfect day.

Music, as from a celestial place,
lingers in the breeze. Love beckons

on this summer's day in every shrub and song
upon faces, like lilies in the light.

Together, hand-in-hand,
vows are spoken, hope-filled words

in a garden—
splendid, green

To Life

How beautiful to have seen her on that day
before her last. She sat in the front row
as you accompanied the musicians in the band.
When singing erupted from the crowd,
I saw her clap her hands, tap her feet,
look over her shoulder at the rest of us,
glad we enjoyed the music as much as she did.
A single yellow flower adorned
the summery hat she wore;
the scarf around her shoulders
was pale green, the color of her eyes.

On her first outing after many months
of being housebound, I'm glad it was warm
in the mid-day sun, that the music filled
the outdoor stage, that there was laughter
all around. I remember that you
glanced several times in her direction,
adoration in your gaze. How beautiful
to have watched as you held her in esteem
to have seen her
as you saw her on that day.

Trespassing

I am a trespasser
at the beach—the first

to come upon its melancholy
after the storm has passed.

Brushstroked by wind and rain
imprints have been forming

like beads of sweat
or falling tears upon the sand.

Quiet looms.

I want to shoulder this remorse
to own this sadness

but just as I cannot know
the grief of a dear friend

whose husband of many years
has died a sudden death

I cannot understand
the mystique—the mourning

of this moment . . .
how all of nature

appears to have
borne this loss.

Words

Some—when softly spoken—are like kisses;

others, cocoons that cradle babes.

Learn to lean on those which heal the

broken-hearted; make meals of those which satisfy

like bread. Explore the ones which gently whet

the senses, a little over time, like summer rains.

They challenge and confront our inhibitions;

instill within a thirst for noble gains.

Some, like nesting sparrows, need be careful

with a brood too young to spread their wings

in flight, but for those to whom the season

beckons, may they impart their wisdom,

their delight. Those that fly too freely from

their coffers, may spew poison from their darts

to rob men's joy. So reprehensible are these,

they ought not be spoken; learn resistance

when tempted to employ. May those with power

to chasten or transform us, abide in rich

abundance through our years, and all the rest

not worth the air that breeds them

fall empty at every turn upon deaf ears.

Written in the Sand

A walk along a sprawling beach
shows shapes of tracts, divergent—
a graphic map lies beneath my frame
dotted with absurdities

Observing different prints
in the sand, I notice two
one left by a delicate foot
another by an athletic shoe

Shaping the bare foot's impression
is a row of tiny ovals;
largest imprint to my left—
an egotistical toe

All rise above an hourglass
a fleshy ball, taut heel
next to the rugged designs
left behind by outerwear

There are cells of blocks & pyramids
a maze of peaks & ridges
parallel lines & squares
wide spans of dissecting bridges

Depicted here before me,
fragments of others' journeys
vagabond chits pressed in the sand—
more than random curiosities

Footprints intended to chart a course
spawn steps of beachcombers before me,
Destinations "certain" as they walked,
though incoming tides engulfed them

Winds and waves wash away
these steps, but in this moment
remind me to shower with love
all those I love
before my days are over

T heresa Hickey is a free-lance writer, poet and lifelong learner who was born and raised in Boston, Massachusetts. A former community reporter for local newspapers, she wrote publicity for Salem State University's Creative and Performance Arts Center events.

When she retired from public service, she realized how much she missed the students and wondered how she might remain connected to them. She began to focus on personal writing projects by participating in the Pelican Bay Women Writers and the Writers Forum of Naples, Florida, where she and her husband of 54 years spend the winter. Prior to writing *Shy*, she published two other chapbooks of poems, *Raising the Child*, and *Sighs of a Gracious Nature*. Her work has appeared in numerous journals and anthologies and earned an EnnyWriters Award from *Naples Magazine*.

As the mother of four, grandmother of seven, she believes her husband, children and grandchildren continue to teach her something new every day. They inspire her to write about faith, family and friends and by so doing, she discovers more about herself and humanity.

She encourages the work of other writers by presenting workshops such as the one she developed for Hodges University—"Creativity Knocks." As a communicant of St. Mary's (MA) and St. John the Evangelist Churches, she believes in giving back, so proceeds from her chapbooks support area soup kitchens, shelters for abused women, the arts, and other nonprofits.

CPSIA information can be obtained
at www.ICGtesting.com
Printed in the USA
BVHW071712220120
569913BV00001B/61